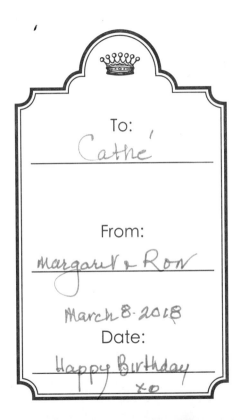

To:

Cathé

From:

Margaret & Ron

March 8·2018

Date:

Happy Birthday

xo

Keep Calm and Pray

© 2013 Christian Art Gifts, RSA
        Christian Art Gifts Inc., IL, USA

Designed by Christian Art Gifts

Images used under license from Shutterstock.com

Printed in China

ISBN 978-1-4321-0892-2

Christian Art Gifts has made every effort to trace the ownership of all quotes and poems in this book. In the event of any question that may arise from the use of any quote or poem, we regret any error made and will be pleased to make the necessary correction in future editions of this book.

16 17 18 19 20 21 22 23 24 25 – 22 21 20 19 18 17 16 15 14 13

Keep Calm and Carry On

In late 1939, after the outbreak of World War II, the British Government commissioned a number of morale-boosting posters that would be displayed across the British Isles during the testing times that lay ahead. The first two posters were posted in public places across Britain.

The third and final poster of the set simply read "Keep Calm and Carry On". The plan in place for this poster was to issue it only upon the invasion of Britain by Germany. As this never happened, the poster was never officially seen by the public.

Nearly 60 years later, a bookseller stumbled across a copy hidden amongst a pile of dusty old books bought from an auction. He put the poster up in the store and was amazed at the response.

It is wonderful to think that all these years later, people still find it so appealing and reassuring. And it is even more fitting when we think of how we can trust God and confidently pray even in the most difficult times, knowing that He is with us and will carry us through.

Grant me, O Lord my God,
a mind to know You,
a heart to seek You,
wisdom to find You,
conduct pleasing to You,
faithful perseverance in
waiting for You,
and a hope of finally
embracing You.
Amen.

Thomas Aquinas

Prayer has a mighty power
to sustain the soul in every
season of its distress
and sorrow.

Charles H. Spurgeon

The more you pray,
the easier it becomes.
The easier it becomes,
the more you will pray.

Mother Teresa

One of the best ways
to get on your feet is
to first get on your knees.

Anonymous

God will either give you
what you ask, or
something far better.

Robert Murray M'Cheyne

"Ask and it will be given to you; seek and you will find; knock and the door will be opened to you. For everyone who asks receives; the one who seeks finds; and to the one who knocks, the door will be opened."

Matt. 7:7-8

Pray, and let God worry.

Martin Luther

Don't worry about anything;
instead, pray about
everything. Tell God what you
need, and thank Him
for all He has done.

Phil. 4:6

He who kneels the most,
stands the best.

Dwight L. Moody

The Holy Spirit helps us in our
weakness. For example,
we don't know what
God wants us to pray for.
But the Holy Spirit prays for us
with groanings that cannot
be expressed in words.

Rom. 8:26

Prayer is an earnest and
familiar talking with God.

John Knox

The best prayers have often
more groans than words.

John Bunyan

"Pray, so that you will not
give in to temptation.
For the spirit is willing,
but the body is weak!"

Matt. 26:41

What can be more excellent
than prayer; what is more
profitable to our life;
what sweeter to our souls;
what more sublime, in the
course of our whole life,
than the practice of prayer!

St. Augustine

"Whatever you ask for in prayer, believe that you have received it, and it will be yours."

Mark 11:24

In the morning, prayer is the
key that opens to us the
treasures of God's mercies
and blessings; in the evening,
it is the key that shuts us
up under His protection
and safeguard.

Henry Ward Beecher

"Whatever you ask in
My name, that I will do, that
the Father may be glorified
in the Son. If you ask anything
in My name, I will do it."

John 14:13-14

It is the prayer of faith that moves the hand of God.

Angus Buchan

Prayer is not learned in a
classroom but in the closet.

E. M. Bounds

The earnest prayer of
a righteous person has great
power and produces
wonderful results.

James 5:16

Keep praying to get
a perfect understanding
of God Himself.

Oswald Chambers

Pray in the Spirit at all times
and on every occasion.
Stay alert and be persistent
in your prayers for all
believers everywhere.

Eph. 6:18

If the only prayer we say
is "thank you" that
would be enough.

Meister Eckhart

Continue earnestly
in prayer, being vigilant
in it with thanksgiving.

Col. 4:2

Prayer unites the soul to God.

Julian of Norwich

In every place of worship,
I want men to pray with holy
hands lifted up to God, free
from anger and controversy.

1 Tim. 2:8

Prayer does not change God,
but it changes him who prays.

Søren Kierkegaard

Pray for all people.
Ask God to help them;
intercede on their behalf,
and give thanks for them.
Pray this way for kings
and all who are in authority
so that we can live peaceful
and quiet lives marked by
godliness and dignity.

1 Tim. 2:1-2

I have so much to do that
I spend several hours in prayer
before I am able to do it.

Martin Luther

Confess your sins to each
other and pray for each other
so that you may be healed.

James 5:16

The Christian on his knees
sees more than the
philosopher on tiptoe.

Dwight L. Moody

The end of the world is coming soon. Therefore, be earnest and disciplined in your prayers.

1 Pet. 4:7

Some people pray just
to pray and some people
pray to know God.

Andrew Murray

May the words of my mouth
and the meditation of my
heart be pleasing to You,
O LORD, my rock and
my Redeemer.

Ps. 19:14

God is the best listener and
you don't need to shout,
nor cry out loud. Because
He hears even the very silent
prayer of a sincere heart.

Anonymous

Prayer is absolutely necessary
to a man's salvation.

J. C. Ryle

"Call to Me, and I will answer
you, and show you great
and mighty things,
which you do not know."

Jer. 33:3

Oh! It is a glorious fact,
that prayers are
noticed in heaven.

Charles H. Spurgeon

God requires us to exercise
our faith and believe that He
can and will answer prayer.

Angus Buchan

Is prayer your steering
wheel or your spare tire?

Corrie ten Boom

Evening and morning
and at noon I will pray,
and cry aloud, and
He shall hear my voice.

Ps. 55:17

More tears are shed over
answered prayers than
unanswered ones.

Mother Teresa

"In this manner, therefore, pray: Our Father in heaven, hallowed be Your name."

Matt. 6:9

More things are wrought
by prayer than this
world dreams of.

Alfred, Lord Tennyson

Answer me when I call to You, O God who declares me innocent. Free me from my troubles. Have mercy on me and hear my prayer.

Ps. 4:1

God does nothing but by
prayer, and everything with it.

John Wesley

I set my face toward the Lord
God to make request by
prayer and supplications.

Dan. 9:3

Wishing will never be
a substitute for prayer.

Ed Cole

This is the confidence
we have in approaching
God: that if we ask
anything according
to His will, He hears us.

1 John 5:14

When I cannot read, when I cannot think, when I cannot even pray, I can trust.

Hudson Taylor

The eyes of the Lord
watch over those who do
right, and His ears are
open to their prayers.

1 Pet. 3:12

The only way to
heaven is prayer.

Madame Guyon

Rejoice always, pray without
ceasing, in everything give
thanks; for this is the will of
God in Christ Jesus for you.

1 Thess. 5:16-18

When I pray for another
person, I am praying for God
to open my eyes so that I can
see that person as God does.

Philip Yancey

"You will call on Me and come and pray to Me, and I will listen to you. You will seek Me and find Me when you seek Me with all your heart."

Jer. 29:12-13

The point of asking is that you
may get to know God better.

Oswald Chambers

"Whatever things
you ask in prayer,
believing, you
will receive."

Matt. 21:22

The fewer the words,
the better the prayer.

Martin Luther

I cry to You for help, LORD;
in the morning my prayer
comes before You.

Ps. 88:13

God always has an open
ear and a ready hand, if you
have an open and ready
heart. Take your groanings
and your sighs to God
and He will answer you.

Charles H. Spurgeon

Hear my cry, O God,
listen to my prayer; from
the end of the earth I call to
You when my heart is faint.

Ps. 61:1-2

One song can change
a moment, one idea can
change a world, one step
can start a journey,
but a prayer can
change the impossible.

Anonymous

Every great movement
of God can be traced
to a kneeling figure.

Dwight L. Moody

O Lord, please hear my
prayer! Listen to the prayers
of those of us who delight
in honoring You.

Neh. 1:11

O Lord GOD, remember me,
I pray! Strengthen me, I pray.

Judg. 16:28

Our prayer and God's mercy
are like two buckets in a well;
while one ascends,
the other descends.

Arthur Hopkins

You, beloved, building
yourselves up in your most
holy faith and praying in
the Holy Spirit, keep yourselves
in the love of God, waiting
for the mercy of our Lord Jesus
Christ that leads to eternal life.

Jude 20-21

To be a Christian without
prayer is no more possible
than to be alive
without breathing.

Martin Luther

Talking to men for God is a great thing, but talking to God for men is greater still.

E. M. Bounds

Our prayers lay the track
down on which God's power
can come. Like a mighty
locomotive, His power is
irresistible, but it cannot
reach us without rails.

Watchman Nee

Jesus Christ carries on intercession for us in heaven; the Holy Ghost carries on intercession in us on earth; and we the saints have to carry on intercession for all men.

Oswald Chambers

Don't pray when you feel like it. Have an appointment with the Lord and keep it. A man is powerful on his knees.

Corrie ten Boom

Prayer is the acid test
of devotion.

Samuel Chadwick

A man may study because his brain is hungry for knowledge, even Bible knowledge.
But he prays because his soul is hungry for God.

Leonard Ravenhill

The neglect of prayer is a
grand hindrance to holiness.

John Wesley

Prayer – secret, fervent,
believing prayer – lies at the
root of all personal godliness.

William Carey

I have seen many men work without praying, though I have never seen any good come out of it; but I have never seen a man pray without working.

Hudson Taylor

If Christians spent as much
time praying as grumbling,
they would soon have
nothing to grumble about.

Anonymous

Whatsoever we beg of God,
let us also work for it.

Jeremy Taylor

If I raise my voice may it be
only in praise. If I clench my
'fist, may it be only in prayer.
If I make a demand, may it
be only of myself.

Max Lucado

The more you pray, the less you'll panic. The more you worship, the less you worry. You'll feel more patient and less pressured.

Rick Warren

Where there is not faith
and confidence in prayer,
the prayer is dead.

Martin Luther

Any concern too small
to be turned into a prayer
is too small to be made
into a burden.

Corrie ten Boom

To pray is to mount on eagle's wings above the clouds and get into the clear heaven where God dwells.

Charles H. Spurgeon

We tend to use prayer as a last resort, but God wants it to be our first line of defense. We pray when there's nothing else we can do, but God wants us to pray before we do anything at all.

Oswald Chambers

For the happy man prayer is only a jumble of words, until the day when sorrow comes to explain to him the sublime language by means of which he speaks to God.

Alexandre Dumas

God will answer your prayers
better than you think.
Of course, one will not always
get exactly what he
has asked for.

Fanny Crosby

The wise man in the storm
prays to God, not for safety
from danger, but for
deliverance from fear.

Ralph Waldo Emerson

We have to pray
with our eyes on God,
not on the difficulties.

Oswald Chambers

Prayer is faith in God,
not faith in prayer.

Anonymous

Whether we like it or not, asking is the rule of the Kingdom. If you may have everything by asking in His name, and nothing without asking, I beg you to see how absolutely vital prayer is.

Charles H. Spurgeon

Prayer is not monologue,
but dialogue. God's voice
in response to mine is its
most essential part.

Andrew Murray

A habit of prayer is one
of the surest marks of
a true Christian.

J. C. Ryle

When the clock strikes it is
good to say a prayer.

Jeremy Taylor

Don't forget to pray today
because God did not forget
to wake you up this morning.

Oswald Chambers

To clasp the hands in
prayer is the beginning
of an uprising against the
disorder of the world.

Karl Barth

We can be tired, weary and emotionally distraught, but after spending time alone with God, we find that He injects into our bodies energy, power and strength.

Charles Stanley

Pray and doubt,
do without. Pray and
believe, humbly receive.

Anonymous

The finest of God's blessings is
to be found in secret prayer.

Charles H. Spurgeon

Answered prayer is the interchange of love between the Father and His child.

Andrew Murray

Prayer is the exercise
of drawing on the
grace of God.

Oswald Chambers

Prayer opens the heart to God, and it is the means by which the soul, though empty, is filled by God.

John Bunyan

There are thoughts which
are prayers. There are
moments when, whatever
the posture of the body,
the soul is on its knees.

Victor Hugo

Prayer is that act in
Christianity in which there is
the greatest encouragement.

J. C. Ryle

As for methods of prayer,
all are good, as long
as they are sincere.

Victor Hugo

Pray the largest prayers.
You cannot think a prayer so
large that God, in answering
it, will not wish you had
made it larger. Pray not for
crutches but for wings.

Phillips Brooks

Prayer without study would
be empty. Study without
prayer would be blind.

Karl Barth

Oh, will you pray?
Stop now and pray,
lest desire turn to feeling
and feeling evaporate.

Amy Carmichael

Prayer is nothing else
than being on terms of
friendship with God.

Teresa of Avila

We never know how God
will answer our prayers,
but we can expect that
He will get us involved in
His plan for the answer.

Corrie ten Boom

Our hearts, our hopes,
our prayers, our tears, our
faith triumphant o'er our
fears, are all with Thee –
are all with Thee!

Henry Wadsworth Longfellow

The least little remembrance
will always be the most
pleasing to Him. One need
not cry out very loudly; He is
nearer to us than we think.

Brother Lawrence

Only that prayer which
comes from our heart can
get to God's heart.

Charles H. Spurgeon

Prayer is asking for the rain
and faith is carrying
the umbrella.

Anonymous

Time spent in prayer
is never wasted.

François Fénelon

Prayer will never do our work
for us; what it will do is to
strengthen us for work
which must be done.

William Barclay

Prayer only from the
mouth is no prayer.

Proverb

Do not face the day until you have faced God in prayer.

Anonymous

Goals not bathed in prayer
or brought in humility before
the Lord turn out to be
downright useless. They don't
go anywhere. They don't
accomplish anything.

Charles R. Swindoll

When we don't pray,
we quit the fight. Prayer keeps
the Christian's armor bright.
And Satan trembles
when he sees the weakest
saint upon his knees.

William Cowper

When our will wholeheartedly enters into the prayer of Christ, then we pray correctly.

Dietrich Bonhoeffer

Life is fragile,
handle with prayer.

Anonymous

Do what you can and pray
for what you cannot yet do.

St. Augustine

The greatest tragedy of life
is not unanswered prayer,
but unoffered prayer.

F. B. Meyer